Benjamin Ide Wheeler

The Life of the Ancient Greeks

Bibliography and syllabus of Cornell university lectures

Benjamin Ide Wheeler

The Life of the Ancient Greeks
Bibliography and syllabus of Cornell university lectures

ISBN/EAN: 9783337036348

Printed in Europe, USA, Canada, Australia, Japan

Cover: Foto ©ninafisch / pixelio.de

More available books at **www.hansebooks.com**

THE

Life of the Ancient G.

BIBLIOGRAPHY AND SYLLABUS

OF CORNELL UNIVERSITY LECTURES.

BENJAMIN IDE WHEELER.

ITHACA, N. Y.
1890.

ABBREVIATIONS.

BD.—Baumeister, Denkmäler des Klassischen Altertums. 3 vols. (1888).

BE.—Büchsenschütz, Besitz und Erwerb im griechischen Alterthume (1869).

CURTIUS—Curtius, Ernst. History of Greece. 5 vols.

GROTE—Grote, George. A History of Greece. 12 vols.

GK.—The Life of the Greeks and Romans (trans. from the third German edition).

HB.—Hermann, Lehrbuch der griechischen Privatalterthümer, 3d edit. (1882); edited by Blümner.

LS.—Blümner, Leben und Sitten der Griechen. 3 vols. (1887).

MHb.—Handbuch der Klassischen Altertums-wissenschaft herausgegeben von Dr. Iwan Müller (1885-90).

PE.—Boeckh, Public Economy of the Athenians (transl. from Die Staatshaushaltung der Athener).

TT.—Blümner, Terminologie und Technologie der bildenden Künste. 4 vols. (1874-87).

THE LIFE OF THE ANCIENT GREEKS.

Lecture I. The Physical Geography of Greece.

Tozer, Lectures on the Geography of Greece (1873) ; Tozer, Classical Geography (Appletons' Liter. Primers) (1877); Bursian, Geographie von Griechenland, 2 vols. (1862); Grote, History of Greece, Part II chap. i; Curtius, History of Greece, I chap. i; Hermann-Blümner, Griech. Privatalterthümer, pp. 8 ff. ; Abbott, History of Greece, I chap. i; Lolling, Müller's Handb. der Altertumswissenschaft, III 99 ff. ; Wordsworth, Greece, pictorial, descriptive and historical.—On climate : Baedeker's Greece, Introd. pp. 29 ff. ; Wachsmuth, Die Stadt Athen im Altertum, I 100 ff. ; Partsch, Das Klima von Athen, Meteorol. Zeitschr, 1884, pp. 473 ff.

The location of Greece as a whole in relation to the sea and to other lands — The mountain ranges — Elevation of mountains — Plains — Rivers — The coast-line — The comparative extent of the land — Soil — Climate.

Lecture II. The Physical Geography of Greece.

(CONTINUED.)

Beside the works already cited : Curtius, Alterthum und Gegenwart, II 22 ff. ; Hehn, The Wanderings of Plants and Animals (Transl. of Kulturpflanzen und Haustiere); Williams, Views in Greece, 2 vols., illustr. ; v. Falke, Greece and Rome, illustr.

The historical significance of location and climate — Products of the soil — Characteristics of Greek scenery.

Lecture III   Characterization of the Greek People.

St. John, Hellenes, I 29 ff. ; Felton, Greece, ancient and modern,
I 271–309; Mahaffy, Social Life in Greece, ¹228 ff. ; HB. pp. 31–37 :
Schmidt, L., Die Ethik der alten Griechen, 2 vols. (1882).

Physical characteristics — Standard of beauty among the
Greeks — Moral and intellectual characteristics — Modera-
tion — Susceptibility toward the beautiful — Fineness of feel-
ing — Sentiment of friendship — Humanity and inhumanity
— Mental alertness — Avarice — Untruth.

Lecture IV.   The Population.

Boeckh, Public Economy of the Athenians, Book I chap. vii ;
Clinton, Fasti Hellenici, ²II 468–484 ; Beloch, Bevölkerung der grie-
chisch-römischen Welt (1886).—For the states : Gilbert, Handbuch
der griech. Staatsalterthümer, 2 vols. (1881). For the colonies and
leagues : Gilbert, II 397 ff.

Estimates of the population of Greece, of Attica, of Athens
— Methods of determination — Division into tribes — States
— Colonies — Early leagues — Other unifying influences :
likeness of speech, community of religion, contrast with the
life and manners of the orientals.

Lecture V.   The Modern State and People of Greece.

Fallmerayer, Geschichte der Halbinsel Morea (1830); Welchen
Einfluss hatte die Besetzung Griechenlands durch die Slaven auf das
Schicksal der Stadt Athen ? (1835) ; Sanders, Volksleben der Neu-
griechen (1844) ; Leake, Travels in the Morea, 3 vols. (1830) ; Leake,
Travels in Northern Greece, 4 vols. (1835) ; Dodwell, Classical and
Topographical Tour through Greece, 2 vols. (1819) ; Ross, Grie-
chische Inselreisen, 4 vols. (1840) ; Curtius, E., Peloponnesos, 2 vols.
(1851); Felton, Greece, ancient and modern, II 249 ff. ; Schmidt, B.,
Das Volksleben der Neugriechen und das hellenische Alterthum

(1871); Wachsmuth, C., Das alte Griechenland im neuen (1864); Mahaffy, Rambles and Studies in Greece, 2d edit. (1878); Snider, A Walk in Hellas (1883); Baedeker's Greece, by H. G. Lolling, Introd. pp. 31 ff. (1889); Bent, The Cyclades (1885); Krumbacher, Griechische Reise (1886); Wyse, Impressions of Greece (1871); —— On the language; Boltz, Die hellenische oder neugriechische Sprache (1881); Vincent and Dickson, A Handbook to Modern Greek (1881).

The controversy concerning the race-connection of the present population of Greece — Various incursions and immigrations of alien populations — Evidences of unbroken line of connection with ancient Greece to be found in various myths, superstitions, and religious observances, in various popular usages and customs, in the language — Characteristics of the people — Financial and industrial interests — Political affairs — The church — The language.

Lecture VI. Attica.

Lolling, MHb., III 110–121; Curtius und Kaupert, Karten von Attika; Wordsworth, Greece, pp. 65 ff.; Hertzberg, Athen historisch-topographisch dargestellt (1885) chap. i; Baedeker, Greece, pp. 104 ff.; Mahaffy, Rambles and Studies, chaps. vi, vii.

Mountains — Plains — Rivers — Extent of Plains — Coast line — Climate — Vegetation — The harbors of Phaleron and Peiraeus.

Lecture VII. Athens.

Wachsmuth, Die Stadt Athen im Altertum, vol. I (1874); Lolling, MHb. III 290–335; Milchhöfer, BD. s. v. Athen; Hertzberg, Athen; Curtius und Kaupert, Atlas von Athen; Harrison and Verrall, Mythology and Monuments of Ancient Athens (1890); Mahaffy, Rambles and Studies, chaps. iii–v; Gregorovius, Geschichte der Stadt Athen im Mittelalter, 2 vols. (1888).

Outline history of the city — The walls — The gates — The monuments of the lower city, following in general the description of Pausanias, the market-place and buildings near it, the southeastern quarter, the Ilissos district, the street of tripods, the precinct of Dionysos and the theatre, the Asklepieion, the Odeion of Herodes Atticus, the Pnyx.

Lecture VIII. The Acropolis.

Lolling, MHb. III 335-352; Baedeker's Greece, 55 ff.; Boetticher, Die Akropolis; Michaelis, Der Parthenon; Bohn, Die Propyläen der Akropolis zu Athen; Kekulé, Die Reliefs an der Balustrade der Athena Nike; Stuart and Revett, The Antiquities of Athens, 4 vols., smaller edit. 1 vol.

Shape and extent — History — The Propylaea — The temple of Athena Nike — Objects between the Propylaea and the Parthenon — The Parthenon — The Erechtheion.

Lecture IX. The Greek Family; Marriage and the Wedding.

HB. pp. 251-278; GK. pp. 190-195; Becker's Charicles, Excursus to Scene xii; St. John, Hellenes, II 1 ff.; Felton, Greece, I 343 ff.; Schreiber, Kulturshist. Bilderatlas, I, Taf. lxxxi; Müller, MHb. IV, 1, pp. 446 ff.; Blümner, BD. s. v. Hochzeit; Blümner, LS. I 150 ff.; Smith's Dict. of Antiquities s. v. Matrimonium. On the Modern Greek usages: Wachsmuth, Das alte Griechenland im neuen, pp. 81-105, and Sakellarios, Die Sitten und Gebraüche der Hochzeit bei den Neugriechen verglichen mit denen der alten Griechen (1880).—On the development of the monogamous family system: McLennan, Primitive Marriage (1876); Morgan, Ancient Society (1878); McLennan, The Patriarchal Theory (1885); Bachofen, Das Mutterrecht; Lubbock, The Origin of Civilization (1870); Schurman, The Ethical Import of Darwinism, chap. vi.

Position of the family in human society — Development of the monogamous family system — Importance of an under-

standing of the Greek family relations — Character of the
marriage relation in Greece — The marriage contract — The
wedding — The Modern Greek wedding.

Lecture X. The Life of the Women.

HB. pp. 64–75; GK. pp. 185 f.; Mahaffy, Social Life in Greece,
pp. 52 ff., 142 ff., 274 ff.; Müller, MHb. IV, 1, pp. 448 ff.; Donaldson, Women in Ancient Greece, Contemp. Review, July, 1878 and
March, 1879; Blümner, LS. I pp. 167 ff.; Smith's Dictionary of Antiquities, s. v. Tela, Fusus; St. John, Hellenes, I 369 ff., II 28 ff.; Göll,
Kulturbilder ³I 250 ff.; Becker's Charicles, Exc. to Sc. xii; BE. pp.
292 f.; Schreiber, Bilderatlas I, Taf. lxxxii and lxxxiii; Haley, The
Social and Domestic Position of Women in Aristophanes, Harvard
Stud. in Class. Philol. I, Art. xi (1890).

Contrasts between the position of women in the Homeric
age, in the classical period, and in the Hellenistic period —
Restrictions upon the appearance of women outside the home
— Life at home — Occupations: spinning, weaving, etc.
(For dress and toilet, vid. Lectt. xv, xvi, xvii) — Character
of Greek women — The Hetairai.

Lecture XI. The Children.

HB. pp. 75–80, 278–301; GK. pp. 195–197; Müller, MHb. IV, 1 pp.
448 d. ff.; Becker, Charicles, Exc. ii to Sc. i (ed. Göll); Mahaffy, Old
Greek Education, pp. 9–23, 32–57; Grasberger, Erziehung und Un-
terricht II, 1 pp. 28 ff.; Smith's Dict. of Antiq. s. v. Amphidromia,
Nomen; BD. s. v. Aussetzen, Ammen, Wickelkinder, Kinderspiele,
Schaukeln; Mahaffy, Social Life in Greece, pp. ⁶163 ff.; Richter,
Spiele der Gr. und Rom. (1887).

Relation to family authority — Mutual responsibility of
parent and child — Birth — Naming — Nursing — Food —
Games and toys — Earliest education — The ephebes.

Lecture XII. The Slaves.

Richter, Die Sklaverei im griechischen Alterthum (1886); Büchsenschütz, Besitz und Erwerb im klassischen Alterthume, pp. 104-
208; Becker's Charicles, Exc. to Sc. vii; Boeckh, PE., see index
s. v. Slaves; IIB. pp. 80 ff.; Gilbert, Handbuch der griech.
Staatsalt-
erthümer, I 31-36, 163-168, II 287-294; Busolt, MHb. IV, 1 pp. 10
ff.; Smith's Dict. of Antiq. *s. v.* Servus; Blümner, LS. III 174 ff.

Numbers — Legal status — The philosophy of slavery —
Differing condition at different periods — The Spartan Helots
— The Athenian slaves — Their relation to masters — Occu-
pations — Punishments — Emancipation — Nationality —
Prices of slaves.

Lecture XIII. The Greek House.

GK. pp. 73-76, 78-84; HB. pp. 143 ff.; Becker's Charicles, Exc. to
Sc. iii; Müller, MHb. IV, 1, pp. 339 ff.; Smith, Dict. of Antiq. *s. v.*
Domus; Winckler, Die Wohnhaüser der Hellenen; Lange, Haus und
Halle; Blümner, BD. *s. v.* Haus; Göll, Kulturbilder [3]III 1, ff.

The insignificance of private houses in the city during the
classical period — Materials of these houses — Size — General plan — Surroundings of house — Entrance — Porter —
Court — Various rooms — Second floor — Roof — Stoves —
Decoration of walls — Development of house architecture in
the Hellenistic period — The Homeric house.

Lecture XIV. The Furniture of the House.

GK. pp. 134-160; Müller, MHb. IV, 1, pp. 376-395; Becker's Charicles, Exc. ii to Sc. viii (Göll); St. John, Hellenes II 97 ff.; Blümner, Das Kunstgewerbe im Alterthum, II 2-154; Weiss, Kostümkunde I, 1, 855 ff.; BD. *s. v.* Tische, Sessel, Fussbank, Betten, Kissen,
Truhen, Lampen, Leuchter; Smith's Dict. of Antiq. *s. v.* Mensa, Lec-
tus, Sella, Thronus, Amphora, Crater, Cyathus, Cantharus, Patera,

Candelabrum ; Buchholz, Die homerischen Realien II, 2, pp. 138 ff. ;
Miller, Die Beleuchtung im Altertum (1885) ; Schreiber, Bilderatlas I,
Taf. lxxxvi.

Couches — Pillows — Mattresses — Chairs — Tables — Jars
— Vases — Jugs — Pots — Drinking vessels — Lamps — The
furniture of the Homeric house.

Lecture XV. Clothing.

HB. pp. 172 ff. ; GK. pp. 160-170 ; Becker's Charicles, Exc. to Sc. xi ;
Müller, MHb. IV, 1, pp. 395 ff.; Blümner, LS. I 11-60; BD. *s. v.*
Kleidung, Chiton, Chlamys, Himation, Gürtel; Smith's Dict. of An-
tiq. *s. v.* Tunica, Pallium, Peplum, Fibula, Chlamys, Exomis ; Weiss,
Kostümkunde I, 1, 700 ff. ; Böhlau, De re vestiaria (1885) ; Studniczka,
Beiträge zur Geschichte der altgriechischen Tracht (1886) ; Buchholz,
Homerische Realien II, 2, pp. 260-274 ; Helbig, Das homerische Epos
von den Denkmälern erlaütert, pp. 115 ff. ; Smith, J. M., Ancient
Greek Female Costume (2d edit. 1883) ; Hope, Costumes of the An-
cients (1812) ; Schreiber, Bilderatlas I, Taf. lxxxiv.

Costume and climate — Costume and civilization — The
clothing of the primitive Greeks — Clothing in the Homeric
age — The introduction of the tunic for men — The period
from Homer to the Persian wars — The classical period —
Special garments : πέπλος, φᾶρος, χλαῖνα, χιτών, ἱμάτιον, ἐξωμίς,
χλαμύς, θολία — The girdle — The color of garments — Ten-
dencies of fashion in the Hellenistic period.

Lecture XVI. Dress for the Head and Feet.

GK. pp. 170-178 ; Blümner, LS. I 60-90 ; Müller, MHb. IV, 1, pp.
426-433 ; Becker's Charicles, Exc. to Sc. xi ; Blümner, BD. *s. v.* Haar-
tracht, Barttracht, Kopfbedeckung, Fussbekleidung; Smith's Dict.
Antiq. *s. v.* Coma, Barba, Pileus, Calceus, Sandalium, Cothurnus ;
Buchholz, Hom. Realien II, 2, pp. 274-279.

Treatment of hair among men in the heroic age — The
elaborate frisure of the Ionico-Asiatic |civilization (7th–5th
century) — The temperate style of the classical age — The
Laconomania — The beard at different periods — The history
of shaving — Barbers and barber-shops — Hats — Styles of
wearing the hair among women — Head-dresses — Sandals
and shoes.

Lecture XVII. The Toilet and the Bath.

HB. pp. 200 ff. ; Blümner, Kunstgewerbe im Altertum II 127 ff. ;
Becker's Charicles, Exc. iii to Sc. viii ; Müller, MHb. IV, 1, pp. 444
ff. ; Blümner, LS. I 178 ff. ; St. John, Hellenes II 65 ff. ; Smith, Dict.
Antiq. s. v. Balneae ; BD. s. v. Baden, Spiegel, Schminken, Sonnen-
schirm, Fächer.—Cn Ornaments, etc., cf. Müller, MHb. IV, 1, pp. 433
ff.; GK. pp. 178 ff.

The bath in Homeric times — In classical times — Public
fountains and baths — Oil — Perfumes — Rouge — Jewelry
and ornaments.

Lecture XVIII. Food and Drink.

HB. pp. 214–235 ; Becker's Charicles, Exc. to Sc. vi ; Müller, MHb.
IV, 1, pp. 441 ff.; Blümner, LS. II, 34 ff.; PE. chaps. xv, xvi, xvii ;
Blümner, TT. I, pp. 1 ff.; St. John, Hellenes II 125 ff.

General characteristics of the Greek cuisine — The preparation of meal — Different sorts — Varieties of bread — Leav-
en — Cakes — Vegetables — Oil — Meat — Fish — Eggs —
Cheese — Wine — Varieties — Method of preparation and use.

Lecture XIX. Table Usages.

GK. pp. 264 ff.; HB. pp. 235 ff.; Becker's Charicles, Exc. to Sc. vi;
Smith's Dict. Antiq. *s. v.* Coena, Symposium; Müller, MHb. IV, 1,
pp. 445 *b* and *c*; Blümner, LS. II 29–34, 36–45; Mahaffy, Social Life
in Greece, chap. ⁵xi; BD. *s. v.* Mahlzeiten, Symposion, Kränze, Kot-
tabos, Gaukler; Schreiber, Bilderatlas I, Taf. lxxvi and lxxvii; Göll,
Die griech. und röm. Küche, Kulturbilder ³II 74 ff.

Arrangement of table and seats at different periods — Service — The courses — Table manners — Dishes — Drinking
customs — The symposia.

Lecture XX. The Cost of Living.

Boeckh, PE. chap. i–xxi; BE. pp. 347 ff.

Inadequacy of all direct comparisons of ancient money val-
ues with our own — Variations in the value of gold and sil-
ver — Wages and incomes — Profits of trade — Price of houses
— Price of grain — Of bread — Of wine — Of oil — Of meat
and other table supplies — Of clothing — Estimated mini-
mum cost of living compared with the known rate of wages
— Cost of living among the wealthier.

Lecture XXI. The Daily Life.

HB. pp. 121 ff.; Blümner, LS. II, 1 ff.

Conditions in Athens best known — Difficulty of judging
to what extent they are peculiar — Peculiar conditions in
Sparta — Divisions of the day at Athens — Clocks — Morn-
ing hours : ablutions, toilet, first meal — Visits — Marketing
— General appearance of street, houses, and shops — Market-
place — The assembly — The courts — Other public service

— The festivals — Noon — The noon-day meal — The public baths — Wine shops and gambling houses — Dinner — Symposium.

Lecture XXII. Sickness, Physic, and Physicians.

Häser, Lehrbuch der Geschichte der Medicin, ²I 62 ff.; Encyclop. Britannica *s. v.* Medicine; Smith's Dict. Antiq. *s. v.* Medicus, Medicina; Smith's Dict. of Biography and Mythology *s. v.* Hippocrates, Galenus, Aesculapius; HB. pp. 351 ff.; Becker's Charicles, Exc. to Sc. viii; Mahaffy, Social Life in Greece, ²290 ff.; St. John, Hellenes III 201 ff.; Blümner, LS. II 62 ff.; Müller, MHb. IV, 1, pp. 458 *b* and ff.; BD. *s v.* Aerzte, Apotheken.—On the cult. of Asklepios: Milchhöfer, BD. I 194 ff.; von Wilamowitz, Isyllos von Epidauros, Philol. Untersuchungen, IX (1886); Köhler, Mittheilungen des deutschen archeol. Inst. zu Athen, II 171 ff., 229 ff.; Baunack, Studien I, 1, pp. 109 (Inscriptions of Epidauros); Curtius, E., Nord und Süd, April, 1877, pp. 95 ff.

Three-fold connection of modern medical science with the Greek — Surgery and physicians in Homer — The cult of Asklepios — Its relation to later medical tradition — Relics of the Asklepieia of Athens and at Epidauros — The inscriptions of Epidauros — Hippocrates — Medical ethics — Writings — Hippocrates to Galen — Medicine venders at Athens — Doctors — Remedies.

Lecture XXIII. Death and Burial.

GK. pp. 287-293; HB. pp. 361-387; Müller, MHb. IV, 1, pp. 261 *c* and ff.; Blümner, LS. II 73 ff.; St. John, Hellenes III 414-440; Becker's Charicles, Exc. to Sc. ix; Schreiber, Bilderatlas I, Taf. xciv f.; Stackelberg, Die Gräber der Hellenen, illustr. (1883); Smith, Dict. Antiq. *s. v.* Funus; BD. *s. v.* Ausstellen, Bestattung, Aschengefässe, Gräber, Totenkultus; Century Magazine, April, 1882, pp. 836 ff.; Wachsmuth, Das alte Griechenl. im neuen, 105 ff.

Graves. —

Death — Care for body — The πρόθεσις — Lament — Funeral procession — Service at grave — Funeral Feast — Methods of burial — Coffins — Tombs and monuments.

Lecture XXIV. Society and Social Entertainment.

HB. pp. 500 ff.; St. John, Hellenes II 204 ff., 170 ff.; Mahaffy, Social Life in Greece, 46 f., 102 ff., 312 ff.; Müller, MHb. IV, 1, pp. 478 b and ff.; Blümner, LS. II 37–61; Ohlert, Rätsel und Gesellschaftsspiele der alten Griechen (1886).

Social opportunities — Social companies — Conventional manners — Responsibility of host — Music — Conversation — Riddles — Stories — Games — Jugglers — Dancers — Jesters.

Lecture XXV. The Greek Religion.

Roscher's Lexikon der griech. und röm. Mythologie; Welcker, Griech. Götterlehre, 3 vols. (1862); Preller, Griech. Mythologie, 2 vols., 3d edit. (1875); Nägelsbach, Homerische Theologie (1840); Coulanges, The Ancient City, introd. and first six chapters; Mahaffy, Social Life in Greece, chap. xii; Grote, Part I, chap. xvi; Hermann-Stark, Lehrbuch der gottesdienstlichen Alterthümer; Blümner, LS. II p. 155 ff.; St. John, Hellenes I 349 ff.; Abbott, E., The Theology and Ethics of Sophocles, Hellenica, pp. 33 ff.; Curtius, E., Die Idee der Unsterblichkeit bei den Alten, Alterthum und Gegenwart, I 121 ff.; Smith, R., The Religion of the Semites, Lect. I and II (1890); Göll, Toleranz, Sektirerei und Proselytenmacherei, Kulturbilder [3]I 278 ff.; Packard, Studies in Greek thought, pp. 1 ff.

Peculiarities in the relation of the individual Greek to his religion — Nature worship — Its conception of deity — Development of attributes — The theogony — Development of the personality of Apollo — Dionysos — Athene — Hermes — Ancestor worship — Family religion — Influence of the rise of philosophy — The religious spirit of the fifth and fourth centuries at Athens.

Lecture XXVI.   The Greek Worship.

Beside the works cited under preceding : Seemann, Die gottesdienstlichen Gebräuche der Gr. und Röm.; Stengel, MHb. V, 3, pp. 1 ff.;
Schreiber, Bilderatlas I, Taf. xi–xvi.

Altars — Temples — Priests : selection, training, appearance, life, duties — Diviners and magicians — Oracles — Sac-
rifice ; its idea, its forms — Prayer — The mysteries — Festivals.

Lecture XXVII.   The Greek Theory of Education.

Grasberger, Erzichung und Unterricht im griech. Altertum, 2 vols.
(1864–1881) ; Schmidt, Geschichte der Pädagogik, vol. I (1873) ; Mahaffy, Old Greek Education (1882) ; Wilkins, Essay on National Education in Greece (1873) ; Browning, O., Introduction to the History of
Educational Theories, (1881), chap. i ; Packard, On Plato's System of
Education, Studies in Greek Thought, pp. 65 ff.; Nettleship, The
Theory of Education in Plato's republic, Abbott's Hellenica, pp. 67
ff.; Newman, The Politics of Aristotle, vol. I, introd. 344 ff.

Importance of an understanding of these theories — Concerning theories of education in general — Greek idea of the
purpose and aim of education compared with the views of
modern educators — Subjects for instruction — Methods of
instruction.

Lecture XXVIII.   Schools and Teachers.

Beside works cited under preceding : Becker's Charicles, Exc. ii to
Sc. i ; St. John, Hellenes I 164 ff.; BD. *s. v.* Schulen, Pädagogen ;
Blümner, LS. I 113 ff.; Müller, MHb. IV, 1, pp. 451 ff.; HB. pp. 311
ff.; Schreiber, Bilderatlas I, Taf. lxxxix ff.; GK. pp. 197 ff.

Lack of public provision — Age of attendance — Time of
day — Vacations — School-rooms — Apparatus — Object
teaching — Arithmetic — Numbers of pupils — Teachers —
Courses — Methods — The higher education — Development
of universities.

Lecture XXIX. Athletics.

Buchholz, Homerische Realien II, 1, 288 ff.; GK. pp. 212 ff., 115 ff.;
Becker's Charicles, Exc. to Sc. v; Mahaffy, Old Greek Education, 25
ff.; Mahaffy, Social Life in Greece, 336 ff.; Müller, MHb. IV, 1, pp. 451 c
and ff.; Blümner, LS. II pp. 94 ff.; St. John, Hellenes I 189 ff.; BD.
s. v. Gymnastik, Hanteln, Ringkampf, Diskoswerfen, Werfen mit
Speeren, Wettlauf, Fünfkampf, Faustkampf, Pankration, Athleten.;
Smith, Dict. Antiq. s. v. Gymnasium, Halteres, Stadium, Discus, Luc-
ta, Pancratium, Cestus; HB. pp. 341 ff.; Schreiber, Bilderatlas I,
Taf. xxi f.; Bintz, Die Gymnastik der Hellenen (1878); Krause, Gymnastik und Agonistik der Hellenen, 2 vols. (1841); Jäger, Die Gymnastik der Hellenen (1881); Haase, Ersch und Grüber Encyclop. s. v.
Palästra.; Bötticher, Olympia pp. 89 ff.; Grasberger, Erziehung und
Unterricht, vol. I, chaps. i and iii.

Relation to education — Relation to religion — Relation to
art — Palaestra — Gymnasium — Preparation for exercise —
Bath — Chariot race — Boxing — Wrestling — Foot-race —
Quoits — Lance-throwing — Leaping — Ball-games — Decline
of gymnastics in professionalism.

Lecture XXX. Music.

GK. pp. 199 ff.; St. John, Hellenes I 184 ff.; Blümner, LS. II 138 ff.;
HB. pp. 317 ff.; BD. s. v. Musik, Flöten, Saiteninstrumente; Müller,
MHb. IV, 1, 452 b and c; Schreiber, Bilderatlas I, Taf. vii; Mahaffy,
Old Greek Education, 36 ff., 61 ff.: Westphal, Die Musik des griech.
Altertums (1883); Girard, L'éducation athénienne pp. 185 ff. (1889).

Value of the Greek word 'music' — The rhapsodes —
Music in education — The Greek scale — The modes —

Stringed instruments — Wind instruments — Clanging instruments.

Lecture XXXI. The Theatre.

Klein, Geschichte des Dramas, vols. I and II (1865); Moulton, The Ancient Classical Drama (1890); Jebb, Primer of Greek Literature, pp. 69 ff.; Donaldson, the Theatre of the Greeks, 6th edit. (1849); Hermann-Müller, Griech. Bühnenalterthümer (Hermann's Lehrbuch III, 2) (1886); Oehmichen, Das Bühnenwesen der Griech. und Röm. MHb. V, 3, pp. 222 ff. (1890); Opitz, Schauspiel und Theaterwesen der Griech. und Römer (1889); Haigh, The Attic theatre, pp. 101 ff. (1889); Articles by Harrison and Haigh in Classical Review, IV 274 ff. (June, 1890); Harrison-Verrall, Mythology and Monuments of ancient Athens, pp. 271 ff. (1890); Arnold, BD. *s. v.* Theatergebaüde, Milchhöfer, BD. *s. v.* Athen, pp, 190 ff.; GK. pp. 121 ff.; Wheeler, J. R., Papers of the American school of classical studies, I 121–179; Schreiber, Bilderatlas I, Taf. i, ii.

Rise and development of the drama in outline — Beginnings of theatre - building — Vitruvius — The orchestra — The stage — Present controversy concerning the stage in early theatres — Seats of spectators — Passages — Entrances — Dimensions — Acoustics — Remnants of the theatre at Athens — At Epidauros — Roman theatres.

Lecture XXXII. The Dramatic Representations.

From works cited above: Hermann-Müller, pp. 107 ff.; Oehmichen, pp. 191–222, 248 ff.; Schreiber, Taf. iii–v; GK. pp. 275 ff.; Opitz, pp. 125 ff.; Haigh, pp. 65–100; 164 ff.; and also, Becker's Charicles, Exc. to Sc. x; BD. *s. v.* Theatervorstellung, Trauerspiel, Lustspiel, Chor, Schauspieler; Göll, Kulturbilder, [3]I 320 ff.; Blümner, I.S. III 45 ff.; St. John, Hellenes II 220; Millet, Costumes in the Greek play at Harvard, Century Magazine, Nov., 1881, pp. 65 ff.; Norman, An Account of the Harvard Greek Play, illustr. (1882); Speed-Pryor, The Oedipus Tyrannus, Record of performance in Cambridge, Eng., Nov. 1887.

Time and occasion — Expense and provision therefor —
The Choregus — Preparation and rehearsal — The judges
and the award — The stage, decorations, scenery, and scenic
machinery — The actors — Number — Distribution of parts
— Elocution — Gesture — Costume — Masks — The chorus,
its office — March and dance — Musical accompaniment —
The audience — Did women attend? — Behavior of the audience.

Lecture XXXIII. Agriculture and Stock.

HB. pp. 93–120 ff.; Boeckh, PE. (see table of contents); St. John,
Hellenes II 269 ff.; Blümner, LS. III 144 ff.; Müller, MHb. IV, 1, 466
b and ff.; BE. pp. 293 ff.; BD. *s. v.* Ackerban; Smith's Dict. Antiq.
s. v. Agricultura; Schrader, Prehistoric Antiquities of the Aryan People, Part IV, chaps. ii–v (Transl. of Sprachvergleichung und Urge-
schichte, 2d edit. 1890); Schreiber, Bilderatlas I, Taf. lxiv f.—On the
animals: Keller, Thiere des classischen Alterthums (1887); Imhoof-
Blumer und Keller, Tier- und Pflanzenbilder auf Münzen und Gemmen
(1889); Baranski, Geschichte der Thierzucht und Thiermedicin im
Alterthum (1886); Hehn, The Wanderings of Plants and Animals
(Trsl. 1888).

Primitive agricultural conditions — Family property —
Property-rights — Value of land — Agricultural methods —
The plow — Threshing — Winnowing — Irrigation — Gar-
dens — Wine-culture — Oil-culture — Sheep — Goats — Cat-
tle — Horses — Mules — Dogs — Cats — Other pet animals
— Geese — Pigeons — Cocks — Monkeys.

Lecture XXXIV. Merchants and Trade.

HB. pp. 419 ff., 452 ff.; St. John, Hellenes III 276 ff.; Becker's Charicles, Exc. to Sc. iv; Blümner, LS. III 165 ff.; Müller, MHb. IV, 1,
pp. 473 *b* and ff.; BD. *s. v.* Banken; BE. pp. 356 ff.; Mahaffy, Social
Life in Greece, chap. xiii; Göll, Kulturbilder ³I 134 ff.; Richter, Han-
del und Verkehr (1886).—On book-trade: Göll, Kulturbilder ³II 207
ff.; BE. 571 ff.; Becker-Göll, Charicles, Exc. ii to Sc. iii; Schmitz,
Schriftsteller und Buchhändler in Athen (1876).

Greeks as a trading people — Social and political standing
of the merchant-class — Retail trade — Shops — Common
articles of trade — Commerce and wholesale trade — Materials of commerce — Book trade — Imports and exports —
Banking and bankers — Capital and interest.

Lecture XXXV. Weights and Measures.

Nissen, MHb. I 665 ff.; Hultsch, Griech. und röm. Metrologie, 2d
edit. (1882); Smith's Dict. Antiq. pp. 1225 ff.; HB. pp. 438 ff.

Measures of length — Their historic importance — Development — Relation to other measures — Measures of surface
— Measures of capacity — Of weight — Different Greek
standards and their relation.

Lecture XXXVI. Money.

Head, Historia Numorum (1887); Gardner, Types of Greek coins
(1883); Head, Coins of the Ancients, 2d edit. (1881); BE. pp. 478 ff.;
Stillman, The coinage of the Greeks, Century Magaz. xxxiii, 788 ff.
(April, 1887).

The communication of weight and money standards from
Asia to Europe — The different standards — Conflict of the
Aeginetan and Euboean standards — Beginnings of Greek
coinage — Religious character of early type — Introduction
of portraiture — Symbolism of coins.

Lecture XXXVII. The Arts and Industries.

Blümner, Gewerbliche Thätigkeit der Völker des klassischen Alterthums (1869); Blümner, TT. 4 vols. (1874-87); Büchsenschütz, BE.
(1869); Büchsenschütz, Die Hauptstätten des Gewerbefleisses im
klass. Alterthume (1869); Blümner, Das Kunstgewerbe im Alterthum

2 Abthlg. (1885); St. John, Hellenes III 96–244 ; Göll, Kulturbilder ³I 162 ff.; Blümner, LS. pp. 153 ff.; Müller, MHb. IV, 1, pp. 470 ff.; HB. pp. 400 ff.; Becker-Göll, Charicles, III 93 ff.; BD. *s. v.* Holzarbeit, Tischler, Schmiede, Goldarbeit, Bäckerei, Brot, Schuhmacher, Walker, Thonarbeit, Glas ; Smith's Dict. Antiq. *s. v.* Fullo, Pistor.

Athens as a manufacturing town — Position of the industrial classes — Carpenters — Cabinet-makers — Blacksmiths — Workers in bronze — Goldsmiths — Bakers and cooks — Tanners — Shoemakers — Dyers — Art of Dyeing — Tyrian purple — Potters — Glass-blowers — Barbers.

Lecture XXXVIII. Travel, Inns, Roads, Conveyance.

HB. pp. 479 ff.; Becker's Charicles, Exc. to Sc. i ; Göll, Kulturbilder ³I 38 ff.; Friedländer, Sittengeschichte Roms 'II 85 ff.; BD. *s. v.* Wirtshaüser; Smith's Dict. Antiq. *s. v.* Hospitium ; Curtius, E., Die Gastfreundschaft, Alterthum und Gegenwart I 203 ff.; Curtius, E., Ueber den Wegebau der Griechen, Abhandl, d. Berl. Akad, 1854, pp. 221 ff.——On carriages : BD. *s. v.* Wagen ; Smith's Dict. Antiq. *s. v.* Plaustrum, Frenum ; Buchholz, Hom. Realien II, 1, 217 ff.; GK. pp 248 ff.; Ginzrot, Die Wagen und Fuhrwerke der Griechen und Römer (1817) ; HB. pp. 481 ff.

Hindrances to travel in antiquity — The institution of guest-friendship (ξενοδοκία) — Inns and taverns — Travel in the Roman period — Roads — Homeric vehicles — Wagons — The harness.

Lecture XXXIX. The Army, Armor, and Tactics.

GK. pp. 231 ff.; Schreiber, Bilderatlas I, Taf. xxxiv ff.; Blümner, LS. III 105 ff.; Göll, Kulturbilder, ³I 187 ff.; BD. *s. v.* Festungskrieg, Waffen ; Smith's Dict. Antiq. *s. v.* Exercitus ; Weiss, Kostumkunde, vol. II ; Rüstow und Köchly, Geschichte des griech. Kriegswesens (1852) ; Herrmann-Droysen, Heerwesen und Kriegführung der Griechen (Lehrb. der gr. Antiq. II, 2) (1889) ; Fickelscherer, Kriegswesen der Alten (1888) ; Bauer, Kriegsalterthümer, MHB. IV, 1, 225 ff.; Hel-

big, Das homerische Epos aus den Denkmälern erläutert, pp. 195 ff.;
Jähns, Geschichte des Kriegswesens (1880); Dodge, Alexander, A history of the origin and growth of the art of war from the earliest times
to the battle of Ipsus (1890).—On mercenaries: BE. pp. 350 ff.; Hermann-Droysen, pp. 74 ff.

The organization of the Spartan army — Of the Athenian
army — Employment of mercenaries — The army on the
march — In camp — In battle ; the general method of con-
ducting a battle — Spartan infantry tactics — Spartan cavalry — Athenian infantry tactics — Athenian cavalry — Theb-
an tactics — Innovations of Philip and Alexander — Armor
— Weapons — Fortifications — Heavy Artillery — Siege.

Lecture XL.   The Marine.

GK. 254 ff.; Smith's Dict. Antiq. *s. v.* Navis, Trierarchia ; Blümner,
LS. III 137 ff.; Bauer, MHb. IV, 1, 276 ff.; Hermann-Droysen, Heerwesen und Kriegsführung pp. 271 ff.; Assmann, BD. *s. v.* Seewesen ;
Fickelscherer, Kriegswesen der Alten, pp. 107 ff.; Schreiber, Bilderatlas I, Taf. xlv ff.; Boeckh, Urkunden über das Seewesen des atti-
schen Staates (1840); Breusing, Die Nautik der Alten (1886); Göll,
Kulturbilder, ³I 386 ff.

The oldest ships — Vessels of two or more banks of oars
— Method of rowing them — Rigging for sails — Rudders —
Oars — Anchors — Sea-fights — Harbors and appointments
— Organization of the Athenian navy — The trierarchy.

www.ingramcontent.com/pod-product-compliance
Lightning Source LLC
Chambersburg PA
CBHW021457090426
42739CB00009B/1770